Cambridge Discovery Readers

Level 1

Series editor: Nichol

T0268630

A Little Trouble in Dublin

Richard MacAndrew

CAMBRIDGE
UNIVERSITY PRESS

CAMBRIDGE
UNIVERSITY PRESS

79 Anson Road, #06-04/06, Singapore 079906

Cambridge University Press is part of the University of Cambridge.

It furthers the University's mission by disseminating knowledge in the pursuit of education, learning and research at the highest international levels of excellence.

www.cambridge.org

This American English edition is based on *A Little Trouble in Dublin*, ISBN 978-84-832-3695-6 first published by Cambridge University Press in 2010.

© Cambridge University Press 2010, 2011

First published 2010
American English edition 2011
Reprinted 2016

Richard MacAndrew has asserted his right to be identified as the Author of the Work in accordance with the copyright, Design and Patents Act 1988.

Printed in Italy by Rotolito Lombarda S.p.A.

ISBN 978-0-521-18157-0 Paperback American English edition

Cambridge University Press has no responsibility for the persistence or accuracy of URLs for external or third-party internet websites referred to in this publication, and does not guarantee that any content on such websites is, or will remain, accurate or appropriate.

No character in this work is based on any person living or dead.
Any resemblance to an actual person or situation is purely accidental.

Illustrations by Kevin Levell

Exercises by hyphen

Cover photo montage by Darío Pérez

The publishers are grateful to the following for permission to reproduce photographic material on the cover: istockphoto.com/© Hofmeester (house); istockphoto.com/© Zocha K (banknotes)

Music composed by Elliot Simons and published by Shockwave-Sound.com

Contents

Chapter 1 Funny money   5

Chapter 2 The man with the forged bills   12

Chapter 3 Going after Mr. Green Shirt   16

Chapter 4 A taxi to the police station   22

Chapter 5 A swim in the River Liffey   26

Chapter 6 Talking to the police   30

Chapter 7 A café on O'Connell Street   36

Chapter 8 Back at the hotel   40

People in the story

Andy Lawson: a 13-year-old boy; Kim Lawson's
   twin brother
Kim Lawson: a 13-year-old girl; Andy Lawson's
   twin sister
Ms. O'Brien: Andy and Kim's science teacher
Mr. Green Shirt: Kim sees this man in a shop
Mr. Blue Shirt: a friend of Mr. Green Shirt
Inspector Helen Forrester: a Dublin police officer
Sergeant Tom Brady: a Dublin police officer

BEFORE YOU READ

1 Look at the pictures in Chapter 1. Answer the questions.

1 What does Kim buy at the start of Chapter 1?

....

2 What do Andy and Kim buy at the end of Chapter 1?

....

Funny money

"Isn't it beautiful?" said Andy Lawson to his sister Kim.

"No," replied Kim. "It's not beautiful, and it's not interesting."

Andrew Lawson, always called Andy, looked at his sister. She was 13 and he was 13. They were twins[1] – but they were not the same. He was 170 centimeters tall with short red hair and blue eyes. She was only 160 centimeters tall with long dark hair and big brown eyes. They didn't look the same, and they didn't think the same.

"Kim," said Andy. "Look at it. It's over a thousand years old. Half a million people come here every year. They want to see this because it is very old and very famous."

Andy and Kim were in the city of Dublin in Ireland. Actually, they were in Trinity College in Dublin, and in front of them was the *Book of Kells*, 680 pages of words and pictures, and over a thousand years old.

"Well, I don't think it's beautiful," said Kim. "I'm going to the museum shop." And she walked away.

The shop was in the next room. Kim looked around. There were books and CDs about the *Book of Kells*, and there were Trinity College T-shirts. Kim looked at the T-shirts.

"I like these," she thought. "And they're not too expensive." She took down a red T-shirt and got out some money. Kim waited with the money in her hand. In front of her was a big man with a green Ireland soccer shirt. The shirt was much too small for him, and Kim saw his stomach. Yuck! The man bought a postcard.

"I'm sorry," he said to the salesperson. "I know the postcards are just 75 cents, but I've only got this." There was a 20-euro bill in his hand.

"That's OK," replied the salesperson.

Kim looked at the money in her hand. It was a 50-euro bill and a kind of orange color. In the United States, of course, the money was not the same – dollars not euros.

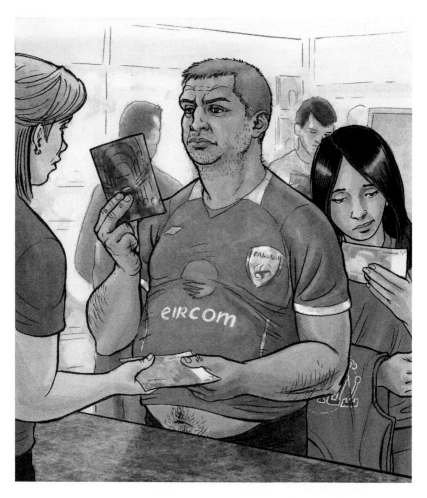

The man walked away. Kim gave the T-shirt to the salesperson.

"That's €14.95, please," said the salesperson.

Kim gave her the 50-euro bill. The salesperson put the T-shirt in a bag and gave it to Kim. Then she gave her €35.05. Kim looked at the bills. The 20-euro bill was blue, the 10-euro bill was red, and the five-euro bill was gray. She put the money in her backpack[2].

Then Andy came into the shop.

"You know, it is beautiful and interesting," he said with a smile on his face, "but not for very long. Come on. I want some ice cream. We've got time. We're meeting Ms. O'Brien at five o'clock, and it's only three now."

Andy and Kim were in Dublin with students from their school in the United States. Their science teacher, Ms. O'Brien, was from Ireland, but she lived in the United States. Every year she took 12 students to Dublin at the start of the summer. The students enjoyed seeing a new city: Dublin is small and friendly, and there is a lot to do. And Ms. O'Brien enjoyed seeing her family.

Andy and Kim walked to Grafton Street, one of Dublin's important shopping streets, and found an ice cream shop. Andy asked for chocolate ice cream. Kim wanted strawberry. Kim gave the salesperson €20, and he looked at the bill. Then he turned the bill over and looked at it again.

"I can't take this," he said.

"Why not?" asked Kim.

"It's not real money. It's forged." He took another 20-euro bill and put it on the shop window. Then he put Kim's bill next to it.

"Look on the left," the salesperson told Kim. "You can see a kind of window on the real money, but there isn't one on yours. Yours is forged. Here."

He gave Kim her bill.

"But –" Kim started to speak.

"Have you got any other money for your ice cream?" the man asked.

Kim found some more money.

"The police say there's a lot of this forged money in the city right now," the salesperson told Kim. "You need to take that one to the police station."

LOOKING BACK

● ●

1 Check your answers to *Before you read* on page 4.

ACTIVITIES

● ●

2 Complete the sentences with either *Andy* or *Kim*.

1 ......*Andy*...... thinks the *Book of Kells* is beautiful.

2 .... has long dark hair and big brown eyes.

3 .... knows how old the *Book of Kells* is.

4 .... goes to the museum shop next door.

5 .... likes the Trinity College T-shirts.

6 .... thinks they've got time for ice cream.

7 .... wants strawberry ice cream.

8 .... gives the salesperson a 20-euro bill.

3 <u>Underline</u> the correct words in each sentence.

1 *Andy / Kim* doesn't think the *Book of Kells* is interesting.

2 Andy and Kim *look / don't look* the same.

3 Andy and Kim *think / don't think* the same.

4 Kim is *160 / 170* centimeters tall.

5 *Over a million / Half a million* people visit the *Book of Kells* every year.

6 The man with the green Ireland soccer shirt gives the salesperson a *20-euro / 50-euro* bill.

7 Kim buys a *Trinity College T-shirt / a CD about the Book of Kells*.

8 Kim's *50-euro / 20-euro* bill is forged.

4 Who or what do the <u>underlined</u> words refer to?

> **the** salesperson   the *Book of Kells* (x2)
> Andy and Kim   a 20-euro bill   Trinity College T-shirts

1 "Isn't <u>it</u> beautiful?" (page 5) *the Book of Kells*

2 Look at <u>it</u>. (page 6) ....

3 "And <u>they</u>'re not too expensive." (page 6) ....

4 Actually, <u>they</u> were in Trinity College in Dublin (page 6)

....

5 Then <u>he</u> turned the bill over and looked at it again.

(page 8) ....

6 Then he put Kim's bill next to <u>it</u>. (page 9) ....

5 Match the questions with the answers.

1 What is very old and very famous? $\boxed{b}$

2 What does the man with the green shirt buy? $\Box$

3 Who does Kim give the forged bill to? $\Box$

4 What does Kim need to take to the police station? $\Box$

a The 20-euro bill.

~~b~~ The *Book of Kells*.

c The ice cream salesperson.

d A postcard.

LOOKING FORWARD

●●●

6 Check (✓) the things you think are true in Chapters 2 and 3.

1 Andy and Kim take the forged bill to the police station. $\Box$

2 Andy and Kim see the man from the Trinity College museum shop again and go after him. $\Box$

Chapter 2

The man with
the forged bills

Out in the street, Kim was angry. She ate some ice cream, then took out the 20-euro bill and looked at it.

"A forged bill!" she said. "Not real! How can I use it now?"

"Listen," said Andy. "Why don't we go and tell Ms. O'Brien about it?"

"Good thinking," replied Kim, and they started walking back to their hotel on Fleet Street.

They got to the hotel at about a quarter to four. They found Ms. O'Brien and told her about the forged bill.

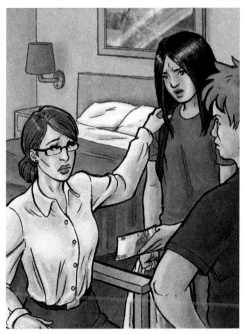

Ms. O'Brien looked at it. Then she looked at Kim's face. It was half angry, half sad.

"Oh, Kim," she said and put a hand on her shoulder.

"It's €20," said Kim. "That's a lot of money to me, and now I can't buy anything with it."

"That's all right," said Ms. O'Brien. She found her purse³ and opened it.

"Here," she said, giving Kim a new 20-euro bill. "You have this. I can call the police." She put Kim's forged bill on the table in front of her.

"Oh, thank you, Ms. O'Brien," said Kim happily. "That is kind of you."

"That's all right," replied Ms. O'Brien. "Now, are you coming to the movies this evening?"

"Yes," answered Kim.

"I don't know," said Andy.

Ms. O'Brien smiled. "Well, we're meeting in the hotel restaurant at five o'clock."

Andy and Kim went to their room and watched TV for half an hour. But Kim didn't really[4] watch. She thought about the forged bill . . . and the Trinity College shop . . . and the man with the green Ireland soccer shirt.

"Yes!" shouted Kim. She turned off the TV.

"Hey," said Andy. "I'm watching that."

"Listen," Kim told him. "The man in the Trinity College shop –"

"What about him?" asked Andy.

"He gave the salesperson a 20-euro bill. The forged 20-euro bill," answered Kim.

"You don't know that," said Andy.

"Yes, I do," replied Kim. "He said, 'This is all I've got' or something like that."

Andy said nothing.

"And he's a fat man, with a green shirt," said Kim. "And the shirt was too small. I saw his stomach."

"Yuck!" said Kim and Andy at the same time. They laughed.

Then Andy said, "OK. The forged bill came from a man in a green shirt, but . . . how many people are there in Dublin? You're not going to find him."

"You're right," replied Kim. She looked angry again. "There are lots of people – but I'd like to find him."

Andy gave her a funny look and turned the TV back on.

At a quarter to five, Kim asked, "Are you coming to the movies, Andy? Come on. Don't watch TV all night."

"Oh! All right," said Andy and turned off the TV. "Which movie are we going to see?"

They went down to the hotel restaurant, and Kim told Andy a little about the movie. Kim stopped near the restaurant. She put her hand on Andy's arm.

"Stop!" she said. "Look!"

At the front of the hotel was a fat man in a green shirt.

"That's him," said Kim quietly[5]. "Mr. Green Shirt."

Mr. Green Shirt had a big box in his hands. He gave the box to the hotel receptionist and said something. The receptionist replied. Andy and Kim tried to listen to the conversation, but they were too far away. Then Mr. Green Shirt turned and left the hotel.

"Come on!" said Kim. "We're going after him."

"We can't!" replied Andy. "We're going to the movies."

"Not now," said Kim. She took him by the hand. "Come on!"

"Sometimes I don't understand my sister," thought Andy. But he ran out of the hotel with her.

Chapter 3

Going after Mr. Green Shirt

Out on the street, they stopped and watched the man in the green shirt walking away.

"Ms. O'Brien's going to be angry," said Andy.

"Not everyone's going to the movies," replied Kim.

"But she thinks you are," said Andy.

"Forget about Ms. O'Brien," said Kim. "This is important."

Kim watched the man. He turned right. Andy and Kim ran after him and turned right, too.

"Don't get too near him," said Kim. "We don't want him to see us."

For 10 minutes, they walked about 50 meters behind the man. First there was Trinity College on their left, then the National Gallery on their right.

Next came Merrion Square. There were houses around the square, and trees and gardens in it.

The man walked up to the front door of a house, opened the door, and went in.

"OK," said Andy. "We can go back now. We've still got time to get to the movies. The movie actually starts at half past five."

"No," said Kim and took him by the arm. "We're going to wait in the gardens."

"Why?" asked Andy. "We can't see him."

"But what's he doing there?" asked Kim. "I want to know."

Andy was angry, but he didn't say anything. "I can't leave my sister here," he thought. They waited and they waited. After 30 minutes, Andy said, "Come on, Kim. He's not coming out again."

"Just five more minutes," said Kim. "Please, Andy."

Andy started to speak, but just then the front door opened and Mr. Green Shirt came out. He walked into the gardens.

"Here he comes," said Kim. Then she saw the look on the man's face. "Oh no!" she said. "He's coming over here. And he's angry."

The man started to run.

"Who are you?" he shouted. "I saw you behind me. Why are you watching me?"

"Run," said Kim. And she and Andy turned and started running. Mr. Green Shirt ran after them.

"Stop!" he shouted. But they didn't. At the end[6] of the gardens, Kim saw a man in a green and red jacket sitting on a big stone. She ran up to him.

"Can you help –" she started to say, but then she stopped.

Andy took her arm. "Come on!" he said. "That's not a real person, stupid. That's a statue of the famous Irish writer Oscar Wilde. There's a picture of it in the hotel."

They started running again. Mr. Green Shirt was behind them, but he wasn't very fast.

"Don't stop," said Andy. They ran out of the gardens and down the street.

After two or three minutes, they stopped and looked back. Mr. Green Shirt wasn't there. Andy looked at Kim. She looked afraid.

"It's all right," said Andy. He put his arm around her. "He's much too slow."

Andy smiled at his sister.

"Come on," he said. "We have to go and tell Ms. O'Brien."

LOOKING BACK

● ●

1 Check your answers to *Looking forward* on page 11.

ACTIVITIES

● ●

2 Underline the correct words in each sentence.

1 Andy *wants* / *doesn't want* to tell Ms. O'Brien about the forged bill.

2 Kim *gets* / *doesn't get* a new 20-euro bill from Ms. O'Brien.

3 In their hotel room, Andy and Kim talk about *Ms. O'Brien* / *the man with the green Ireland soccer shirt*.

4 Andy and Kim *go to the movies* / *go after Mr. Green Shirt*.

5 Andy and Kim wait for Mr. Green Shirt to come out of the *house* / *gardens*.

6 Mr. Green Shirt wants *Andy and Kim to leave* / *to know about Andy and Kim*.

7 Kim stops and talks to *a statue* / *Mr. Green Shirt*.

8 Andy and Kim stop running and look back, but *they don't see Mr. Green Shirt* / *Mr. Green Shirt is still running*.

3 Put the sentences in order.

1 Kim tells Andy about the movie. ☐

2 Kim sees Mr. Green Shirt at the front of the hotel. ☐

3 Andy and Kim tell Ms. O'Brien about the forged bill. ☐ 1

4 Kim runs up to a statue. ☐

5 Mr. Green Shirt runs after Andy and Kim. ☐

6 Andy and Kim run out of Merrion Square and into the street. ☐

7 Andy and Kim watch TV. ☐

8 Andy and Kim wait for Mr. Green Shirt. ☐

4 Are the sentences true (*T*) or false (*F*)?

1 Kim thinks it's good to tell Ms. O'Brien about the forged bill. [T]

2 A 20-euro bill is a lot of money to Kim. ☐

3 Andy is going to the movies in the evening. ☐

4 Andy and Kim listen to Mr. Green Shirt's conversation with the receptionist. ☐

5 Kim thinks that it is important to go to the movies. ☐

6 Andy and Kim walk behind Mr. Green Shirt to Merrion Square. ☐

7 Mr. Green Shirt sees Andy and Kim in the gardens. ☐

8 Mr. Green Shirt is a fast runner. ☐

5 Answer the questions.

1 Who gives the Trinity College salesperson the forged 20-euro bill?

....

2 Why does Kim want to wait in the gardens?

....

3 Why is Mr. Green Shirt angry?

....

4 Whose statue is in Merrion Square?

....

LOOKING FORWARD

● ●

6 Check (✓) the things you think are true in the next three chapters.

1 Andy and Kim don't go to the movies. ☐

2 Ms. O'Brien calls the police. ☐

3 Andy and Kim see Mr. Green Shirt again. ☐

Chapter 4

A taxi to the police station

Ms. O'Brien came back from the movies at half past seven. Kim and Andy went to see her in her room.

"Where were you, Kim?" asked Ms. O'Brien. She looked a little angry. "Why didn't you come to the movies with us?"

"I'm very sorry, Ms. O'Brien," said Kim, "but we've got something to tell you."

"Well?" asked Ms. O'Brien. She didn't smile. "Tell me."

First Kim told Ms. O'Brien about Mr. Green Shirt in the Trinity College museum shop. Then she told her about the house in Merrion Square, and about him running after them. Ms. O'Brien listened to Kim. For a minute or two she looked at her hands and thought. Then she looked up at Andy and Kim.

"OK," she said. "We have to go and tell the police about this. I'm going to call a taxi. You go and wait at the front of the hotel. I'm coming down in just a minute."

"Thank you, Ms. O'Brien," said Kim.

Andy and Kim went down to the front of the hotel. They walked across the street and waited for the taxi.

"Ms. O'Brien is nice," said Kim. "She didn't actually get angry with us."

"No, she didn't. But we're here for two more days," said Andy. "There's still time."

Kim laughed. Not many cars drove down Fleet Street. After five minutes, a taxi turned into the street. It stopped just in front of the teenagers.

"This must be our taxi," said Kim. She walked over to it and opened the back door.

"Is this for Ms. O'Brien?" she asked the back of the driver's head.

"That's right," said the driver.

Kim got into the back. Andy went around the car, got in next to her, and closed the door.

"Ms. O'Brien is coming," said Kim to the driver. She turned and started to say something to Andy, but then saw the look on her brother's face. Andy's eyes were on the driver. Kim looked at the driver, too. Then she saw it. Under the driver's brown jacket. A green shirt!

"Out now," said Andy, and tried to open his door. Kim tried her door at the same time. The back doors didn't open, but the front door did, and a second man got into the car. He was tall and thin. He wore a blue shirt and black pants. He looked back at Andy and Kim. He had black hair and a cold smile.

"You can't get out," he said. "The doors don't open. And nobody can see in . . . the windows are dark."

He turned to Mr. Green Shirt. "Go!" he said. The car started and they drove off.

"What are you doing? Where are you taking us?" asked Kim.

Mr. Blue Shirt turned and looked at Kim. He smiled again. His eyes really were cold.

Chapter 5

A swim in the River Liffey

"Help!" shouted Andy. "Help!"

Mr. Green Shirt turned on the radio. It was loud rock music. Nobody heard their shouts. Mr. Blue Shirt turned around again and looked at Andy and Kim. He didn't say anything. He didn't need to. Andy stopped shouting. The man turned back and watched the road. Andy looked out of the window. Nobody looked in. Mr. Green Shirt drove across the River Liffey and turned right. There were houses on their left and the river on the right.

"Where are these men taking us?" thought Andy. "What are they going to do?" He thought of answers to his questions, and he didn't like them. These men were bad.

"We need to do something quickly," thought Andy. But he didn't know what. He looked at Kim. She didn't look afraid.

"*The Good-bye Game*," she said.

"What?" thought Andy. "What is she talking about? Why is she talking about a movie?" *The Good-bye Game* was a movie about a French cook and his family. It was a very funny movie. But . . .

Mr. Blue Shirt looked around quickly. "Stop talking," he said angrily.

Andy looked at Kim again. He didn't understand. What was important about the movie? Kim closed her eyes slowly. Then she opened them again.

Of course! Now Andy understood. In the movie, the cook is driving down the road with his five-year-old son in the back of the car. The son puts his hands over his father's eyes. The car goes off the road into a tree, and all the doors open. Maybe he and Kim . . .

It was a dangerous[7] thing to do, but they needed to get away from these men. He looked at Kim and closed one eye. She gave him a little smile. Andy closed his hand. Kim watched his hand. One finger came out, then a second, then a third.

At the same time, Andy put his hands over Mr. Green Shirt's eyes, and Kim put hers over Mr. Blue Shirt's. The two men shouted. Mr. Green Shirt took his hands off the wheel, and the car turned fast across the road. The river was now in front of them. Andy and Kim took their hands away quickly. Mr. Green Shirt put his hands back on the wheel. But the car was too fast, and the river was too close.

"Left! Left!" Mr. Blue Shirt shouted. But it was too late. There were shouts and noise in the car and on the street. There was rock music from the CD player. There was more noise, then the sound of the car hitting the water. But the doors didn't open.

Chapter 6

Talking to the police

"Quick! Open the window!" Andy shouted. Quickly he
and Kim opened the back windows of the car and started
to get out. Water started to come in. Cold water. Lots of
it, coming in fast.

The men in the front didn't look around. They just
wanted to get out, too, but the front doors weren't easy to
open. There was too much water.

"Out!" shouted Andy. He and Kim got quickly into the water. They were good swimmers. In minutes they were out of the water and on the street. Back in the river, the men opened the car doors slowly and started to swim away.

"Are you OK?" asked the people on the street. "Do you need a doctor?"

There was a seat near the river. Andy and Kim sat down. A woman started to give Kim her coat. A man in a brown coat took out his phone and called the police. Then Andy looked up the street and saw the blue light of a police station.

"There's a police station up there," he said to Kim. He took her by the hand. "Come on." They started running up the street in their wet clothes.

"Hey! Wait!" called the man in the brown coat. "The police are coming!"

But the teenagers didn't stop. They ran to the police station. The police took away Andy's and Kim's wet clothes and gave them some old ones. Then they put the teenagers in a room and gave them a hot drink and cookies. Two police officers, a man and a woman, came into the room and talked to them. Andy and Kim told them everything.

At 10 o'clock the teenagers were still at the police station. Across the table sat the two officers. The woman, Inspector Helen Forrester, wore a dark blue jacket and pants and a white shirt. The man, Sergeant Tom Brady, wore a light blue shirt and dark blue pants.

"We got to the river too late," Forrester said to Andy and Kim. "The men in the car got away." She put some pictures on the table in front of her.

"It's late now, and I have to call your teacher and tell her you're OK. But first I've got some pictures." She turned them over. "Are any of these the men in the taxi?" she asked.

Andy and Kim started looking at the pictures of men's faces.

After a minute or two, Andy took one and gave it to the inspector. "Here's one," he said. "That's the man with the green shirt."

Then Kim turned a picture around for the inspector to look at. "And here's Mr. Blue Shirt," she said.

Forrester looked at the pictures and gave them to Brady. He looked at them.

"I know these two," he said with a small smile.

"OK," said Forrester to the teenagers. "Now I'm going to call your teacher. What did you say her name was again?"

"O'Brien," replied Kim. "Ms. O'Brien."

Brady looked quickly at Forrester. "Of course," said Forrester. She thought for a minute. "And you say she called us about the forged money on Grafton Street this afternoon?"

"That's right," replied Kim.

Forrester looked at Brady and then back at Andy and Kim.

"Is something wrong?" asked Andy.

"No, no," said Forrester. "There are a lot of O'Briens in Dublin."

She looked at Brady. "Sergeant," she said, "you get their clothes. I'm going to call Ms. O'Brien." Then she looked at the teenagers. "And you two, wait here a minute." The police officers left the room.

Andy looked at Kim. "Why did she say 'There are a lot of O'Briens in Dublin'?" he asked.

"I don't know," replied Kim.

LOOKING BACK

. . . .

1 Check your answers to *Looking forward* on page 21.

ACTIVITIES

. . . .

2 <u>Underline</u> the correct words in each sentence.

1 Andy and Kim see Ms. O'Brien *after / before* the movie.
2 Kim tells Ms. O'Brien about *the statue / Mr. Green Shirt*.
3 *Mr. Green Shirt / Mr. Blue Shirt* is driving the taxi.
4 In *The Good-bye Game* the car drives into a *river / tree*.
5 Andy and Kim put their hands *on the wheel / over the men's eyes*.
6 The men open the *car doors / front windows* and swim away.
7 The police get to the River Liffey *before / after* the men get away.
8 Brady *knows / doesn't know* Mr. Green Shirt and Mr. Blue Shirt.

3 Complete the sentences with the words in the box.

half past seven	five minutes	in minutes
10 o'clock	Mr. Green Shirt	Andy Kim

1 Ms. O'Brien comes back from the movies at *half past seven* .
2 Andy and Kim wait at the front of the hotel for ....
3 .... shouts for help.
4 .... talks about *The Good-bye Game* in the taxi.
5 Andy and Kim get out of the car and onto the street

   ....

6 At .... Andy and Kim are at the police station.
7 Andy gives Inspector Forrester a picture of ....

34

4 Match the two parts of the sentences.

1 What are Andy and Kim doing at the front of the hotel? ☐ b
2 Why can't anybody see in the taxi? ☐
3 Why doesn't Kim look afraid in the taxi? ☐
4 Why does Mr. Green Shirt take his hands off the wheel? ☐
5 Why does Forrester leave Andy and Kim in the room? ☐

a Andy puts his hands over his eyes.
b̶ They're waiting for a taxi.
c She goes to call Ms. O'Brien.
d She's thinking about how to get away from the men.
e The windows are dark.

5 Answer the questions.

1 Where are Andy and Kim at the start of Chapter 4?

....

2 What do Andy and Kim do to the men in the taxi in Chapter 5?

....

3 What are the two police officers going to do at the end of Chapter 6?

....

LOOKING FORWARD

● ●

6 Check (✓) the things you think are true in the final two chapters.

1 Ms. O'Brien comes to the police station. ☐
2 Andy and Kim don't see the men again. ☐
3 Andy and Kim help the police. ☐

Chapter 7

A café on O'Connell Street

At twenty past ten, Ms. O'Brien came into the room at the police station. Forrester and Brady were behind her.

"Oh! Andy, Kim. There you are," she said and put her arms first around Kim, then around Andy.

"Are you all right? The inspector told me everything."

Forrester spoke, "OK, you can go now. You get some sleep. We're going to try and find these men."

Ms. O'Brien looked at the teenagers.

"Are you all right?" she asked again.

"Yes," said Kim, "I'm OK."

"I'm hungry," said Andy.

Ms. O'Brien and the police officers laughed. "Come on!" said Ms. O'Brien. "There's a late night café on O'Connell Street. It's only five minutes from here."

At ten-thirty Kim, Andy, and Ms. O'Brien were in Maguire's Café on O'Connell Street. Kim had another hot drink and some more cookies; Andy had milk and cake. Ms. O'Brien took her phone out of her purse.

"Well, I'm going to call my brother," she said. "No more taxis for us! He can come and get us."

Ms. O'Brien went out of the café and made a short phone call. Then she came back in and sat down again.

"Well, then," Ms. O'Brien looked at Andy. "Did you enjoy seeing the *Book of Kells* this afternoon, Andy?"

"Yes, I did," said Andy, laughing, "but Kim didn't."

"Andy!" said Kim.

"That's all right," said Ms. O'Brien. "Not everyone finds it interesting."

Andy and Kim finished their food and drinks. Then they all stood up and walked to the café door. Ms. O'Brien opened it.

"That's my brother's car over there," she said.

Andy and Kim walked out onto the street. Twenty meters away to the right was a black car. A man in a baseball cap got out. He turned and opened the back door of the car. Someone came up behind them from the left. Then everything happened very fast.

Police officers ran out from everywhere. The man by the car was Mr. Blue Shirt. He turned and tried to run, but he was too slow. Two police officers quickly stopped him. The man behind them was Mr. Green Shirt. Two police officers took his arms.

Andy looked around for Ms. O'Brien. But she was fast. She saw the police and started running up O'Connell Street.

Mr. Green Shirt saw this. "Run, Deirdre, run," he shouted.

Kim looked at Andy.

"How does Mr. Green Shirt know Ms. O'Brien?" she asked. Then she understood.

Chapter 8

Back at the hotel

Kim shouted "Quick!" and started running after Ms. O'Brien.

Andy was behind Kim. Police officers started running behind Andy and Kim. But the teenagers were fast. Kim got to Ms. O'Brien first. She took her left arm.

"Stop!" she shouted. "Stop!"

Ms. O'Brien tried to get away, but Andy took her left arm, and then the police were there. By then it was too late.

* * *

At 12 o'clock that night, Andy and Kim and Inspector Forrester were back at the hotel.

"I phoned your parents and told them everything," she said. "I also spoke to the principal[8] of your school. Two new teachers are arriving in Dublin tomorrow. They're going to take you back home to the United States."

"Thank you," said Andy. "But I still don't understand. How did you know about Ms. O'Brien?"

"We didn't really," Forrester started to reply, "but your Mr. Green Shirt is a man named Fergus O'Brien. There are a lot of O'Briens in Dublin but –"

"But they're from the same family," finished Kim.

"Yes," said Forrester. "Actually, Mr. Green Shirt is Ms. O'Brien's brother. And Mr. Blue Shirt, he's Patrick Donnelly, a friend of theirs. Donnelly and O'Brien make forged money, and Deirdre O'Brien, your teacher, helps them change their forged money for real money. You saw her brother at work. He buys something cheap with some forged money and gets real money back."

"How do you know she helps him?" asked Andy.

"Well, we know that she never called us about your forged €20. Also, her brother left a box here at the hotel this afternoon," said Forrester. "You told us about that."

"That's right," said Kim.

"Well, we found it in her room," said Forrester. "There was €20,000 in it."

Andy and Kim looked at Forrester, their mouths open.

Then Andy asked, "But Mr. Green Shirt and Mr. Blue Shirt? How did they know about us and about the hotel?"

"Ms. O'Brien phoned them," said Forrester. "She told them to come in a taxi and take you away. Her brother Fergus sometimes works for Grafton's Taxis."

"What did they want to do with us?" asked Kim.

Forrester stood up.

"I think it's time for bed," she said, "It's after 12 o'clock."

Andy and Kim stood up, too.

"Yes," said Kim. "I'm tired."

"Me, too," said Andy.

Forrester looked at them. "Your teachers are getting here at midday tomorrow," said Forrester. "What are you going to do before that? Why don't you go and see the *Book of Kells*?"

"We saw that today," said Andy quickly. "It was beautiful, wasn't it Kim?"

Forrester saw the look on Kim's face. "I see," she said. She smiled, too. "You didn't like it much then, Kim."

"No," she said. "I didn't. And I lost €20 when I went there!"

LOOKING BACK

1 Check your answers to *Looking forward* on page 35.

ACTIVITIES

2 Put the sentences in order.

1 Andy, Kim, and Ms. O'Brien go to Maguire's Café. ☐
2 Andy, Kim, and Forrester go to the hotel. ☐
3 The police find forged bills in Ms. O'Brien's hotel room. ☐
4 Andy and Kim learn that Mr. Green Shirt is Ms. O'Brien's brother. ☐
5 Ms. O'Brien goes to the police station. ☐1☐
6 Andy and Kim run after Ms. O'Brien. ☐
7 Ms. O'Brien runs up O'Connell Street. ☐
8 Ms. O'Brien calls her brother. ☐

3 Match the two parts of the sentences.

1 Where does Ms. O'Brien take Andy and Kim? ☐d☐
2 Why does Ms. O'Brien's brother come to take her, Andy, and Kim? ☐
3 Why do police officers run out of everywhere? ☐
4 How do the police know that Ms. O'Brien helps Mr. Green Shirt? ☐
5 How do Mr. Green Shirt and Mr. Blue Shirt know that Andy and Kim are at the hotel? ☐

a They want to talk to Mr. Green Shirt and Mr. Blue Shirt.
b They find forged bills in her hotel room.
c Ms. O'Brien phones them.
d A late night café.
e Ms. O'Brien doesn't want them to take a taxi again.

4 **Are the sentences true (*T*) or false (*F*)?**

1 At the police station, Forrester tells Ms. O'Brien everything. [T]

2 Maguire's Café is near the police station. ☐

3 Ms. O'Brien calls Fergus from Maguire's Café. ☐

4 Kim enjoyed seeing the *Book of Kells*. ☐

5 Mr. Green Shirt sees the police and starts running. ☐

6 Andy and Kim take Ms. O'Brien by the arms. ☐

7 Deirdre O'Brien makes forged bills. ☐

8 Fergus buys things with forged bills and gets real money back. ☐

5 **<u>Underline</u> the correct words in each sentence.**

1 Ms. O'Brien comes into the room at the police station at *ten-thirty* / *twenty past ten*.

2 Andy *isn't hungry* / *enjoyed seeing the Book of Kells*.

3 Mr. Blue Shirt is a *slow* / *fast* runner.

4 *Fergus* / *Patrick Donnelly* sometimes works for Grafton's Taxis.

5 Andy and Kim are going back to the United States with *the police* / *some different teachers*.

6 **Answer the questions.**

1 Why does Ms. O'Brien go out of Maguire's Café?

....

2 Who is Mr. Green Shirt?

....

3 How did Forrester know Deirdre O'Brien works with her brother?

....

Glossary

● ●

[1]**twin** (page 5) *noun*   someone's brother or sister born at the same time as them

[2]**backpack** (page 7) *noun*   a bag you carry on your back

[3]**purse** (page 12) *noun*   a bag carried by a woman with her money, keys, etc., inside

[4]**really** (page 13) *adverb*   actually

[5]**quietly** (page 14) *adverb*   without noise

[6]**end** (page 18) *noun*   when something finishes

[7]**dangerous** (page 27) *adjective*   when something can hurt you

[8]**principal** (page 41) *noun*   the person whose job is to look after all teachers and students at a school